Journey to Being Debt-Free

A Goal for Every Church

Journey to Being Debt-Free
A Goal for Every Church

Dr. Aaron R. Jones

NUVISION PUBLISHING

All scripture quotations are from the King James Version of the Bible. Thomas Nelson Publishers, Nashville: Thomas Nelson, Inc. 1972.

Editor: Dr. Sharon D. Jones
Natasha Anthony

ISBN: 978-0-9961267-5-5

Library of Congress Control Number: 2025926294

NUVISION PUBLISHING

Published by NuVision Publishing
Wilmington NC
nuvisiondesigns.biz

Table of Contents

INTRODUCTION

As a pastor, I am driven by a vital question: What legacy will I leave for the Kingdom of God? Throughout my years in ministry, I have pursued what matters most—preaching the Word with power, reaching the lost, loving people genuinely, and making an impact both locally and globally. These are noble pursuits—worthy goals that reflect the very heart of God. Yet another conviction has grown equally strong within my spirit: the desire to leave behind a debt-free church.

You see, I believe that financial freedom is not simply a matter of good budgeting or strong fundraising—it is about spiritual stewardship and Kingdom vision. A debt-free church is not bound by the limitations of monthly payments or the fear of economic downturns. Instead, it stands as a testimony to God's provision, wisdom, and faithfulness.

When the people of God are free from financial bondage, ministry can flow unhindered, and pastors can lead with boldness rather than burden.

Too often, we, as church leaders, celebrate the spiritual victories while quietly carrying the financial weights that limit our progress. We rejoice over souls saved but grieve under the weight of budget challenges. We dream of outreach and expansion but face the harsh reality of debt that limits our impact.

Yet, I am convinced that God never intended for His church to live in financial captivity. Scripture reminds us that the borrower is servant to the lender (Proverbs 22:7), and I know that the same God who called us to preach freedom to the captives desires to see

His church walk in that same freedom—financially, spiritually, and missionally.

This booklet is born out of that conviction. It is not merely about numbers, budgets, or balance sheets—it is about vision, faith, and obedience. The journey to being debt-free is not just a financial strategy; it is a spiritual journey of trust. It's about teaching our congregations to live within God's principles of stewardship, challenging our leaders to model financial integrity, and inspiring our churches to believe that with God, debt-free ministry is possible.

Imagine the impact of a church that owes nothing to anyone but love. Imagine the freedom to give generously, to build without borrowing, to send missionaries, to meet community needs instantly—without waiting for approval from a bank. Imagine the testimony it would bring to a watching world when the Church declares, “The Lord has provided!”

This is the LEGACY I long to leave—not just buildings, not just memories, but a model of ministry rooted in faith and financial freedom. A debt-free church sets future generations up for success. It positions them to dream bigger, reach farther, and serve

deeper without the chains of yesterday's obligations.

My prayer is that as you read these pages, you will catch the same vision and hear the same call. This is not a journey for one church alone—it's a goal for every church that seeks to honor God fully in every area. Together, we can build churches that stand as living testimonies of God's provision, wisdom, and glory.

Welcome to the ***Journey to being Debt-free***—a journey of faith, discipline, and divine freedom.

NEW HOPE COG

God's People building God's Kingdom

SESSION 1

NEW HOPE'S STORY

<u>Our Journey to Becoming Debt-Free</u>

I want to share a short version of our church's incredible journey toward becoming completely debt-free.

It all began with a prompting from the Heavenly Father. As Senior Pastor, I wanted to position our church so that we would no longer be hindered by financial obligations. In January 2018, I met with our Pastor's Council to present a plan to eliminate our church's debt of $2.5

million. After much prayer, discussion, and careful deliberation, we came into full agreement, passing a unanimous vote to begin this journey using an outside financial resource to help us reach freedom from debt.

At our annual church business meeting, I shared the same vision with our entire congregation. Once again, the response was unanimous—we would move forward together in faith toward becoming financially free.

The resource tool that became a game changer for our journey was an ***Index Universal Life Account (IUL)***. The IUL is an insurance policy placed on me, with the church as both the owner and beneficiary. The church maintained full control over the policy; my role was simply to provide the life coverage. The church paid the monthly premiums, and over time, the policy accumulated cash value, which became a powerful asset in helping us reduce our debt.

DISCLAIMER: An IUL is one financial tool among many possible strategies for church debt elimination. It worked for our specific situation, but may not be suitable for every church. This account is shared for informational and educational purposes only—not as financial advice or a recommendation. Every church's situation is unique. Before implementing any financial strategy, churches should consult with qualified financial advisors, legal counsel, and denominational leadership to determine what is appropriate for their circumstances.

Throughout this journey, our leadership had to make tough decisions regarding staffing, events, and programs. We restructured our budget and regularly reassessed our effectiveness in every area. Unity among leadership was vital. We refrained from filling needed positions in the church to redirect the funds to the debt. I even operated without an assistant for two years—it was a major sacrifice, but I truly believed it was needed.

Although many of the congregants did not realize it. I wanted to set the example that was needed, so that the ministry would know I was not asking them to do something, I was not willing to do. Also, we paused certain programs, redirecting those funds toward principal payments on the mortgage.

However, even in our season of sacrifice, we never stopped serving

our community or the world.

Our nonprofit organization remained open six days a week, continuing to provide Emergency Needs Assistance, Restorative Living, Workforce Development, and Garden Programs. Internationally, we kept building the Outreach House for Children in the Philippines, supporting our churches in Africa, and continuing to bless missionaries around the world.

Communication was another key to our success. Each week, we provided updates on our debt-free progress, keeping the congregation informed and inspired.

In December 2022, we made our first principal-only payment of $26,000, reducing our mortgage balance to just under $2 million. Over the next two-and-a half-years, we borrowed from the IUL to put more than $1 million toward our mortgage.

Then, in May 2025, during our annual business meeting, we issued a faith challenge—to raise $150,000 in three months. ***By God's grace and through the generosity of our people, we met that goal, allowing us to completely pay off the mortgage and plan our***

Mortgage Burning Celebration for November 2025!

In less than three years, God enabled us to pay off nearly $2 million of debt. It took God's plan, prayer, unity, sacrifice, and yes—an IUL. We also invited churches to partner with our vision to be debt-free in 2025. Praise God, churches participated and assisted in the vision along with us.

In future sessions, I'll share the detailed steps, strategies, and lessons learned from this incredible journey.

SESSION 2

"OWE NO MAN ANYTHING"

"Owe no man anything, but to love one another: for he that loveth another hath fulfilled the law." — Romans 13:8

The Apostle Paul's exhortation in Romans 13:8 is often neither quoted nor prioritized in the Body of Christ. Honestly, many churches and church leaders do not place it as a church priority. Simply put, these words, penned by the Apostle Paul, who was led by the Holy Spirit, reveal the heart of

God for His people to walk in freedom and integrity—not bondage and burden.

The nature of debt represents a form of servitude. God uses His Word to enlighten our minds to the position debt places on individuals and the church. Proverbs 22:7 reminds us, *"The borrower is servant to the lender."* When the Church becomes entangled in financial bondage, it limits its ability to move at the pace of the Spirit. Instead of advancing ministry with freedom and boldness, decisions become delayed by obligations and constraints.

God is not a God of lack, but of sufficiency. Ephesians 3:20 says, "Now unto him that is able to do exceeding abundantly above all that we ask or think, according to the power that worketh in us." God's desire is that His Church not only reflect His faithfulness and order, but His abundance. A debt-free church can be the example to the Body of Christ and to the world of what it means to trust in Jehovah Jireh—the Lord who provides.

A church in debt can still show love to the world and operate in love with one another. Paul connects the "owe no man anything" with "but to love one another."

This reveals that financial freedom fuels spiritual effectiveness. When the Church is not bound by debt, it can fully express the love of Christ through giving, outreach, and generosity.

A debt-free church is in a better position to meet community needs without hesitation; support missions both locally and globally; empower families to experience freedom in their own finances; and invest in future generations rather than leaving them with the burden of repayment.

Freedom in finances leads to freedom in ministry. A debt-free church has the capacity to love unconditionally and give generously because it owes only Christ.

SESSION 3

RELEASE THE LIMITATIONS

The vision of God pours into the heart of the pastor and overflows into kingdom assignments. However, the fulfillment of those visions is sometimes delayed—or, in some cases, never realized at all. Most pastors understand the tension between vision and provision. God faithfully gives the vision, but the resources necessary to bring that vision to life must follow. When those resources are hindered by financial strain or debt, even the most inspired plans can become confined.

Debt has a way of changing the atmosphere of a ministry. Instead of the church operating with freedom and creativity, the focus slowly shifts from outreach to in reach—from expansion to survival. Pastors and leaders begin to spend more time maintaining what already exists rather than pursuing what could be. The church that once walked boldly by faith sometimes finds itself walking cautiously by sight, guided more by financial statements than by the Spirit's leading.

If this cycle remains in place long enough, it begins to shape the culture of the entire congregation. Pastors and leaders start to believe that limited progress is normal, that lack is inevitable, and that financial struggle is just part of ministry life. But that is not the abundant life Christ promised His Church. Jesus said, *"I have come that they might have life, and have it more abundantly (John 10:10)."* Debt does the opposite—it drains vitality, restricts vision, and silences momentum. It attacks morale by making ministry feel like a burden rather than a joy. It attacks mission by redirecting attention away from souls and service toward bills and budgets.

When the financial obligations of a church outweigh its spiritual aspirations, the pastor's heart becomes heavy. Dreams that once stirred excitement now bring anxiety. Plans for outreach are postponed. Mission trips are delayed. Building improvements are set aside. In essence, debt becomes a spiritual distraction, pulling the focus of the church away from kingdom advancement and toward mere survival.

However, when a church becomes debt-free, something powerful happens. The atmosphere shifts. Vision begins to flow again. Creativity is renewed. The congregation moves from a place of constraint to a place of confidence. The pastor and leadership team can once again dream with God without the weight of financial limitation. Resources that were once tied to debt can now be redirected to ministry, missions, and outreach.

A debt-free church is a church that can respond quickly to the leading of the Holy Spirit. When God opens a door for opportunity, the church can step through without hesitation or financial fear. Ministry becomes proactive instead of reactive. The church can support families in crisis, sow into missions, invest in the next generation, and bless the community—all without asking, "Can we afford it?"

Becoming debt-free is more than a financial goal—it's a spiritual breakthrough. It restores joy, renews focus, and releases the full potential of the church's mission. When the burden of debt is lifted, the church is no longer limited by what it owes but empowered by what it owns. That freedom allows the body of Christ to move forward in faith, fulfill God's vision, and truly release the limitations.

SESSION 4

UNDERSTANDING STEWARDSHIP

God is looking for the Church to be good stewards over what is placed in our hands. The Bible is clear; God is not looking to send blessings to those who are not looking to be good stewards.

Stewardship precedes God's supernatural increase.

The parable of the talents is found in Matthew 25:14–30. It identifies the significance of good **stewardship**. We are entrusted with resources and expected to use them wisely.

Faithful use of what God gives us will carry a reward. When we are not faithful, by wasting the gifts, the result is loss and disappointment. In other words, nobody wins. Good stewards are responsible and intentional with the resources, gifts, or assignments entrusted to us by our Heavenly Father.

To become debt-free is not just about numbers—it's about alignment with God and His assignment. When our financial practices align with God's Word, we position ourselves for divine favor. **Stewardship** is one of the most neglected forms of worship. **Stewardship** honors God by being faithful to what He gives us.

Churches that walk in good **stewardship** are intentional about creating/analyzing their budgets; spending on kingdom assignments, and they lead by example, teaching members to manage their own finances in godly ways.

A debt-free church doesn't happen overnight—it happens through a commitment to biblical principles and a shared vision among leadership and congregation.

SESSION 5

CREATING TONE SETTER'S

Debt-free is less likely to take place if pastors and ministry leaders do not set the tone for stewardship. People, oftentimes, imitate the priorities and practices of their leaders. When leaders embrace the vision of financial freedom, there is a better chance the congregation will follow.

Church leaders are tone setters and

play a vital role in creating the atmosphere for financial freedom to take place in the life of the church. How they respond to the vision and plans of becoming financially free shapes how members view and handle the resources God entrusts to them. The path to financial freedom in the eyes of the church works best when paved with integrity, transparency, and generosity. This is the framework that creates a culture of responsible stewardship throughout the church.

Good stewardship has the greatest impact when it is modeled from the top. Leaders understand that their accountability, and faithfulness in managing ministry finances begins at home. This becomes the bridge to bring the principles to the Body of Christ. By teaching and living biblical principles of giving, saving, and managing resources wisely, they inspire others to do the same.

> *Church leaders set the spiritual and practical example that stewardship is not just about money, but about managing time, talents, and treasures in a way that honors God and advances His Kingdom.*

When leaders embody this mindset, they cultivate a church community that is trustworthy, generous, and mission-focused.

I will outline more in the coming sessions, but in short, leaders who are tone setters for financial freedom will cast clear vision, display transparency and accountability, and model the way.

Leadership must understand that becoming debt-free is not just a financial campaign—it's a spiritual journey that requires faith, unity, and intentionality.

SESSION 6

LEAVING A LEGACY

A debt-free church leaves behind more than just buildings—it leaves behind a lasting testimony of obedience, faithfulness, and wise stewardship. True legacy is not just found merely in the four walls of a church, but also in the values and vision that outlive the current generation. When a church commits to living debt-free, it proclaims that it trusts in the provision of God more than in the promises of financial systems. It becomes a living witness to the next generation that faith in God's ability to provide is stronger than any dependence on credit or loans.

Pastors and congregations alike carry the responsibility of preparing the way for those who will come after them. Just as the patriarchs of Scripture built altars and monuments to remind future generations of God's faithfulness, a debt-free church serves as a spiritual monument declaring, "God provided." This kind of legacy shifts the focus from financial burden to spiritual freedom. Instead of leaving behind multiple financial obligations, the church leaves behind open doors for ministry, outreach, and mission. The next generation is then free to expand, and to serve without the weight of inherited debt.

When churches are free from financial bondage, they can fully engage in the work of the Kingdom. Resources once tied to interest payments and mortgages can be redirected to advancing the gospel—feeding the hungry, clothing the poor, supporting missionaries, and equipping believers for service. This kind of freedom fulfills Mathew 25. ***Financial freedom is not just a practical goal; it is a spiritual***

statement of faith in action.

Leaving a debt-free legacy doesn't leave the next generation to navigate through financial obligations to do ministry. The work of our Lord and Savior Jesus Christ, who paid the ultimate debt for humanity. ***On the cross, Jesus canceled the spiritual debt we owed—a debt we could never repay on our own.*** When He rose from the dead, He sealed our redemption with eternal victory. Just as Jesus freed us from the bondage of sin, a debt-free church models that same principle of redemption and release. We are no longer slaves—to sin or to financial strain—but free to serve and worship God wholeheartedly.

This act of stewardship is both a reflection of divine grace and a response to it. To be a good steward is to recognize that everything we have belongs to God. Every dollar, every building, every resource entrusted to the church is a tool for His glory. When we manage those resources wisely and avoid unnecessary debt, we honor the One who gave them. It's not just about being financially responsible—it's about being spiritually accountable.

Ultimately, a debt-free legacy is a

testimony that faith works. It's a declaration that God's promises are true and His provision is sure. Future generations will look back and see a people who trusted God completely, who sowed in faith, and who reaped the reward of obedience. They will inherit not a burden, but a blessing—a ministry unshackled and ready to move forward. That is the true legacy every pastor and congregation should desire to leave behind: a living example of what it means to walk by faith and not by sight.

SESSION 7

LEADER PONDER QUESTIONS

1. What do you think God would say about our current financial situation?

2. What areas of our current budget can be modified?

3. What is the best approach to reach our congregation to connect them spiritually and practically with a debt-free vision?

4. What are three small action steps in the next 30 days to begin the journey of financial freedom?

5. What can we put in place at our church to leave a culture of financial freedom so that future generations remain free from financial bondage?

SESSION 8

THE DEBT-FREE PLAN

Part I Synchronize

Moving As One
Toward Being Debt-free

A church wanting to walk into financial freedom becomes a difficult task if there is no unity. Every leader, staff member, and ministry head must be synchronized—aligned in both vision and plan. The journey to becoming debt-free is more than making all the interest and principal payments, it is a shared conviction that honors God with wise stewardship and collective obedience.

Unity, vision, and discipline don't require finances, but they help to align leadership. The senior pastor and leadership team must clearly define the vision and direction, ensuring that every ministry and leader understands the vision and plan going forward. Leaders being unified becomes the motivation for the debt-free journey. The senior pastor cannot be the only cheerleader for financial freedom. Also, every ministry must support the vision of debt-free in word and in deed.

Communicating milestones is key; the church needs to see the hand of God working on the church's behalf to complete the vision of financial freedom. I cannot overestimate the importance of transparency regarding every dollar. Continue to communicate the plan throughout the plan. Transparency builds trust, and trust fuels participation. Celebrating small wins encourages the congregation that you are going in the right direction. Highlight victories: testimonies of generosity, answered prayers, or breakthrough moments. Clarify next steps: what's coming next in the plan and how members can continue to participate through giving, prayer, and faith.

Don't wait until the debt is gone to rejoice—celebrate along the way! Each milestone achieved is a reminder of God's faithfulness and the power of unity. Have recognition moments when major goals are reached. Encourage testimonies from members who have personally experienced financial breakthroughs as they joined in the church's debt-free vision. Use these moments to renew commitment and rekindle excitement for the next phase.

When the church is synchronized operating in unity, there is clear communication, transparency, and momentum builds. The people's faith grows stronger, generosity flows more freely, and the vision of a debt-free ministry becomes not just possible, but inevitable.

SESSION 9

THE DEBT-FREE PLAN

Part II Maximize

Making the Most of Every Resource

Once the vision is clear and the church is unified in purpose, the next step is to maximize every available resource to accelerate the journey toward financial freedom. Becoming debt-free is not simply about cutting back; it's about strategic stewardship in making intentional choices that multiply the impact of every dollar entrusted to the ministry.

Every extra dollar makes a difference. When surplus funds are applied directly to the principal, it reduces the total interest paid and shortens the overall payoff period. Encourage ministries to operate efficiently and return unused budget allocations to the debt reduction fund. Even small, consistent additional payments compound into major progress over time.

When unexpected blessings come – such as special offerings, donations, gifts, or higher-than-expected income – we are to put this toward the principal payments. These moments present divine opportunities to make big steps toward financial freedom. Establish a policy or covenant that a portion (or all) of these unexpected funds will go directly toward debt elimination. This practice aligns with the biblical principle of faithful stewardship—being wise and intentional with every increase God provides.

Encourage members to contribute specifically toward the “Debt-Free Project.” Create an opportunity for the congregation to give; this will empower the congregation to take ownership of the vision. I believe members should give above their regular tithes and offerings; this will make an impact on the church debt. When members see how their contributions bring the church closer to financial freedom, it builds momentum, unity, and faith.

Remain committed to giving to other nonprofits, missions, and community needs. Becoming debt-free should never lead to an inward focus. ***The church must continue to sow outwardly, even while paying off debt.*** This keeps the ministry aligned with God's heart for generosity and compassion. Remember the law of sowing and reaping: as the church continues to bless others, God continues to bless the church.

Generosity must remain a lifestyle, not a season.

Teaching biblical stewardship during the debt-free journey helps members focus on managing their own debt. They become more aware of money management—giving, saving, budgeting, and avoiding unnecessary debt. Encourage transparency and accountability in financial matters, both individually and corporately. When the congregation understands God's design for stewardship, they will not only support the church's debt-free journey but also experience personal financial breakthroughs.

Reinforce that debt elimination does not eliminate generosity.

Freedom from debt is not the finish line—it's a new starting point for greater generosity. The goal is not merely to stop paying lenders but to start investing more deeply in Kingdom work.

Reinforce that once the debt is paid off, the same passion and discipline that drove debt reduction should now drive mission expansion, ministry support, and community transformation.

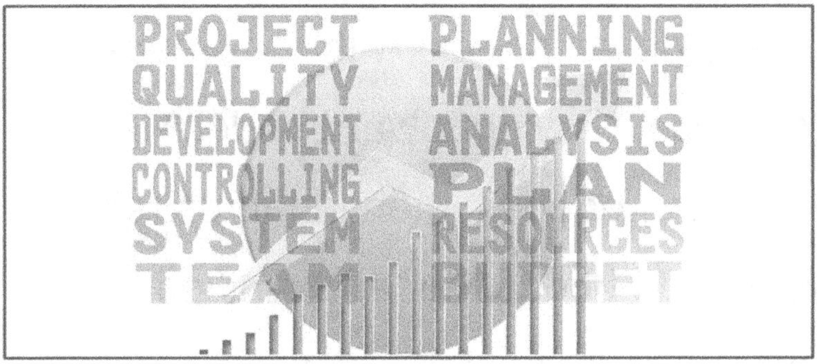

SESSION 10

THE DEBT-FREE PLAN

Part III Minimize
Practicing Wise Restraint on the Journey to Debt-freedom

Just as maximizing income accelerates progress, minimizing unnecessary expenses is just as important to the financial health of the church. Minimizing expenses protects the church's financial health and ensures every dollar is used with maximum purpose. Moving toward a debt-free ministry requires intentional restraint, prayerful budgeting, and unified commitment to stewardship. Minimization isn't about cutting ministry effectiveness—it's about sharpening focus and removing financial waste so that more resources can be directed toward Kingdom work. Refrain from adding more staff while maintaining ministry effectiveness. Personnel expenses often make up a large portion of a church's budget.

A debt-free journey may require a temporary restructuring of roles or redistributing responsibilities. This does not mean compromising the quality of ministry but rather finding creative ways to maximize efficiency. Consider part-time or volunteer leadership roles where appropriate. Cross-train staff and empower capable lay leaders to share ministry responsibilities. Evaluate each position prayerfully, asking, "Is this role essential to our mission right now?" These actions may be difficult, but when handled with transparency and grace, they can free significant funds to accelerate debt repayment.

Limit discretionary or excess spending until the debt is eliminated. **Every**

expenditure should pass the test of purpose: Does this directly advance our mission or debt-free goal? The church can temporarily pause or scale back non-essential projects, upgrades, or activities that are nice—but not necessary. Encourage a culture of contentment and stewardship across all ministries. During the debt-free journey, you may have to delay facility upgrades that are purely cosmetic; reduce ministry-related travel or conference costs; encourage ministries to operate within lean, clearly defined budgets. This season of sacrifice is temporary, but the impact of becoming debt-free will be long-lasting.

In order to be intentional about minimizing expenses, reviewing the church budget should be constant in order to carefully check for inefficiencies. A detailed financial review helps reveal hidden leaks that drain resources over time. Schedule an annual or semi-annual budget review with key leaders. Identify recurring costs that no longer serve the mission. Negotiate better rates for services, utilities, or supplies. Set measurable goals for reducing waste. Every dollar saved brings the church one step closer to freedom. This intentional act reflects both financial responsibility and spiritual maturity toward financial freedom.

SESSION 11

THE DEBT-FREE PLAN

Part IV Prioritize
Establishing the Right Order for Debt-freedom

Becoming a debt-free church does not happen by chance — it requires intentional prioritization. Every ministry, expenditure, and financial decision must align with the ultimate goal of eliminating debt and building lasting financial health. "Prioritize" means putting debt elimination at the forefront of all planning, budgeting, and stewardship decisions until full freedom is achieved. Establish a clear timeline and strategy. To become debt-free, the church must set a specific timeline for paying off obligations and develop a structured strategy to meet that goal. Set a target date for full debt elimination. Create annual and quarterly milestones to measure progress. Assign accountability by having the finance team, pastors, and ministry leaders review and track progress regularly.

Align the annual budget so that debt

reduction remains a top-line priority, not an afterthought. When the church's leadership clearly defines when and how debt will be eliminated, it unites the congregation around a shared vision of financial freedom. Wise stewardship includes using financial tools that strengthen the church's long-term position. One such tool worth considering is an **Index Universal Life (IUL) policy** ***(as mentioned in Session 1).***

While not a replacement for discipline and budgeting, it can be a strategic complement to a debt-free plan. An Index Universal Life (IUL) policy is a life insurance plan that combines protection, growth, and flexibility. It allows the church to accumulate cash value that can be accessed and used strategically for debt reduction and future ministry expansion.

Key Benefits for a Church:

1. Tax-Advantaged Growth (IRS Tax Code 7702) Under IRS Code 7702, the cash value in an IUL grows tax-deferred, and the church can borrow from the policy's cash value tax-free. This makes it a unique financial vehicle for accumulating wealth without triggering

taxable events — a rare advantage among financial tools.

2. <u>Borrow Against the Death Benefit</u> — Tax Free

The church can borrow from the policy's cash value without penalty or taxation, using those funds to pay down debt or fund ministry projects. This provides a source of liquidity without disrupting normal cash flow.

3. <u>Protection from Market Losses</u>

The IUL is linked to a stock market index (such as the S&P 500), but not directly invested in it. This means the church can benefit from market gains while being shielded from market losses — ensuring stable, consistent growth even during economic downturns.

4. Continuous Income Stream

Over time, the policy's cash value can serve as a long-term income source, supporting ongoing ministry operations or emergencies. It becomes a financial "safety-net" that outlives short-term campaigns and budgets.

5. Flexibility and Liquidity

Unlike many traditional investments, an IUL offers access to funds when needed, providing flexibility to address pressing financial needs, fund new initiatives, or accelerate debt repayment.

6. Death Benefit Protection

The IUL also provides a death benefit, ensuring that if the key insured individual (such as the senior pastor or another leader) passes away, the church receives a significant financial benefit. This can secure ongoing ministry continuity and protect the congregation from future financial strain.

Keep debt reduction as a top-line priority. Every financial decision the church makes — from staff hiring to facility upgrades — must be filtered through one primary question: *"Does this help us move closer to being debt-free?"*

This mindset ensures that financial priorities remain aligned with the mission. It creates a culture where faithfulness with resources precedes expansion, and stewardship becomes a spiritual discipline. When the church consistently prioritizes debt elimination — while also investing in tools like the IUL to strengthen its financial base — it builds a future of freedom, stability, and lasting impact. Prioritization means discipline today for freedom tomorrow.

When a church commits to strategic

planning, wise financial tools, and consistent focus, debt-freedom is not just a dream — it becomes a testimony of God's provision and the power of stewardship.

Becoming a debt-free church is more than a financial goal—it is a spiritual journey of faith, discipline, and unity. When a church maximizes its resources, minimizes unnecessary expenses, prioritizes a clear and prayerful strategy, aligns its leadership, and continues to practice generosity, it positions itself for lasting transformation.

SESSION 12

Freedom Outcomes

Becoming a debt-free church is more than a financial goal—it is a spiritual journey of faith, discipline, and unity. When a church maximizes its resources, minimizes unnecessary expenses, prioritizes a clear and prayerful strategy, aligns its leadership, and continues to practice generosity, it positions itself for lasting transformation.

Financial freedom opens the door for greater ministry impact, deeper community engagement, and unhindered obedience to God's vision. As the burden of debt is lifted, the church can move forward with renewed strength—ready to invest fully in Kingdom work and serve as a living testimony of God's provision and faithfulness.

Let this be the season your church declares: *"Owe no one anything, except to love one another (Romans 13:8)."* The journey to debt-freedom is not just about dollars—it's about destiny.

ABOUT THE AUTHOR

Dr. Aaron R. Jones serves as Senior Pastor of New Hope Church of God of Waldorf, Inc. He oversees New Hope COG World Missions which provides mission support to Jamaica, Indonesia, Africa, Philippines, Zambia, and Europe. He also oversees New Hope Church COG Ghana, New Hope COG Uganda, and New Hope Naga Philippines Outreach Center.

Dr. Jones serves the Church of God International Office as Personal Evangelism Coordinator for the Ministry of Evangelism; the International Church of God's Ministry to the Military Board;

the Church of God DELMARVA-DC Regional Council; Coordinator for the Ministerial Internship Program; Chairman of the Ministerial Development Board; Chairman of the Intercultural Advisory Committee; Board of Investigations; and served 2 years on the World Mission's Board.

He is the recipient of the Presidential Lifetime Achievement Award 2025. In his local community, he is the Executive Director of New Hope Community Outreach Services, Inc., a nonprofit organization that provides human services to residents in Charles County, Maryland and the surrounding communities. He serves as End Hunger of Waldorf Board member; Mediation Advisory Council board member; and a Charles County Community Mediator. He served as Former Chief of Chaplains for the Charles County Sherriff's Office and Co-Chair of Religious Affairs Committee of the Charles County NAACP.

Dr. Jones is a Certified Pastoral Counselor with the International Association of Christian Counseling Professionals and a member with the International Coach Federation. He is a Certified SYMBIS Facilitator; a Certified Leader Labs Trainer, and a Certified TTI

Success Insight 12-Driving Forces and DISC Behavior Assessor.

He is the founder and owner of God's Comfort Ministries (GCM) based in Waldorf, MD. GCM provides Christian literature, leadership, coaching, evangelism, discipleship, life insurance, and soul care training. He has published 39 books/workbooks and has recorded two CDs.

Dr. Jones served over 20 years in the Army and retired as a chaplain. He participated in both Operation Noble Eagle (2003) and Operation Iraqi Freedom III (2005). Dr. Jones is happily married to his wife, Sharon, for 28 years.

www.ingramcontent.com/pod-product-compliance
Lightning Source LLC
LaVergne TN
LVHW022312200926
848481LV00004B/1309
* 9 7 8 0 9 9 6 1 2 6 7 5 5 *